Event Plann

Simplified Guide To Become A Successful Event

Planner/Manager (Tips For Beginners And Seniors)

Amoo O. Olaleye

1

Table of Contents

INTRODUCTION

Creating exceptional events is a challenging yet rewarding endeavor. To decorate a room, it's not enough anymore: it's time to learn how to make a lasting impact for your company, your attendees, and most importantly, your professional identity.

Let's face reality. Most events are boring. But they don't have to be. This highly actionable, fast-reading guide is chock-full of unconventional, un-borrifying tools, ideas, and strategies to help you design more captivating and unmissable events for less money and in less time.

Discover how to effectively put on a successful event series that can generate revenue and become your main business or generate leads and exposure to your main business.

Gain valuable insights from interviews with practicing event planners, and stay on track with checklists, worksheets, and other resources.

Successful events do not just fall together; they result from hard work, creativity, awareness, and careful attention to detail - every detail.

Whether you're a veteran, newbie, or "accidental" event planner, you'll learn fresh strategies to smartly select speakers, manage logistics, set a content road map, as well as plan and execute rave-worthy events of all types. Inspired by decades of delivering everything from large-scale corporate events to multiple TEDx gatherings, this fun, practical book will transform how you plan your next event, no matter how large or small. Get the book and get value in successful:

- Planning, budgeting, and strategy

- Guests and target audience

- Promoting and marketing events

- Location, venue, and travel logistics

- Food, drink, entertainment, and themes

- Security, health and safety, permissions, insurance, and the likes

- Tips for building a career in event planning and management

CHAPTER 1

Who is an event planner?

A professional who organizes and coordinates special events such as weddings, ceremonies, corporate gatherings, fundraisers, and corporate parties. Also known as an event planner or event specialist, an event planner is also called an event coordinator. They organize budgets, coordinate transportation and accommodations for guests, and find dates. The specific tasks of an event planner depend on many factors, such as the event's size, type, and the planner's education. An event planner also has other duties.

- To understand the purpose of an event, we meet with our clients

- Plan the event's scope, including the cost, time, place, and program

- Inspection of places to ensure they meet client's needs.

- To coordinate details, speak with the staff on-site.

- Monitor event activities to ensure that the client and guests are happy

- Examining and authorizing payment

Average salary

The salary of an event planner will depend on many factors, including the organization's size and type, location, and their experience level.

The standard salary in the U.S. $15.60 an hour

Some salaries start at $7.25 to $42.60 an hour.

Event planner requirements

Event planners can choose from the following career paths:

- *Education:* A Bachelor's degree in Business,

Communications, or Public Relations is required to become an event planner. A degree is not necessary to apply for entry-level positions, but you should have at least one or two years of experience in this field.

- *Training:* Companies prefer candidates who have had formal training. Many event planners will receive training in the field from someone who has worked in a similar position. You might shadow a senior planner to help you learn the ropes and then take on your tasks.

- Many universities and colleges offer programs in event planning training. These programs typically last between two and four years and include both lectures and hands-on event planning.

- *Certificates:* Many event planners are experts in one type of event. No matter what their area of expertise, event planners can be distinguished by obtaining a professional certification. These are the most popular certifications in this field:

- **_Certified Special Events Professional (CSEP):_** The International Live Events Association (ILEA) offers the CSEP certification to event professionals who have demonstrated the ability, knowledge, and skills required to execute all aspects of a special event. Candidates must have at least minimum of three years of experience in event planning, and they must pass the CSEP exam to be eligible for this certification.

- **_Certified Meeting Professional (CMP):_** This designation is offered by the Events Industry Council (EIC) to event planners who are experts in organizing conventions and meetings. The CMP exam covers meeting management.

- *Certified Professional in Catering and Events (CPCE):*

- The CPCE certification program is organized by the National Association for Catering and Events. It's a nationally recognized program that allows event planners to become experts in the catering, hospitality, and events industries. Candidates must successfully complete a training program before taking the exam to become CPCE certified.

- *Certified Government Meeting Professional (CGMP):* The CGMP certification, jointly developed by the Graduate School at USDA (SGMP) and the Society of Government Meeting Professionals(SGMP), is for planners and suppliers whose work is regulated under the federal government. This is the most prestigious designation for organizers of government meetings.

13

- *Certified Conference and Events Professional (CCEP):* The American Society of Association Executives (ASAE) offers the CCEP certification to professionals who wish to improve their ability to manage an organization. Candidates must have at least minimum of two years' experience and a bachelor's/master's degree in a related field to collegiate events and conferences. They also need to submit a letter and a resume and then complete the CCEP program.

Skills

These are the skills event planners need to be successful in their job:

Attention to detail: Event planners should be able to identify and correct minute details. This could include spelling errors and guest preferences.

Organization: Event planners need to be

organized. Event planners must be able to keep track of multiple tasks, vendors, and to-do lists while still keeping clients happy.

Networking: Event planners require a wide range of event professionals to help them plan events. This is because the event industry is heavily people-driven. Planners will use this network to make their events memorable for their clients.

Communication: Event planners must be able to listen and speak clearly. They must be able to listen to their clients and offer their ideas and suggestions.

Creativity: Planning an event requires creativity. The job involves designing a unique theme and finding affordable decorating solutions that fit within a limited budget.

Interpersonal: Event planners need to be comfortable with maintaining and building relationships with vendors. This will make it easier for them to plan future events.

Problem-solving: Even though events are often scheduled according to a schedule, unexpected circumstances can happen. Event planners need to be flexible and resourceful to make quick decisions.

Event planners work in a supportive environment: Event planners work in an office to perform administrative tasks such as booking hotels and reserving venues for events. Event planners working in large hotels and convention centers may share a workspace with other event planners, answering phones and registering guests. Event planners may work longer hours as the event date approaches. Event planners might need to work fast depending on how many events they are responsible for.

Event planners who plan significant events, such as film screenings, annual conventions, or regional job fairs, may visit clients' workplaces to discuss their requirements. Event planners may visit clients at their

16

headquarters to discuss requirements, such as the guest list, hours and dates of the event, and keynote speakers' names and contact information.

How to be an event planner

These are the steps that you should take to be a successful event planner.

1. Earn a bachelor's degree

A bachelor's degree is not required but can help event managers who are interested in a career as event managers to get a better job and negotiate a better salary. Marketing and hospitality management are two relevant majors.

2. Gain work experience

Event planners might start in a similar field to get started in the industry. To get a feel for what it is like behind the scenes of events, they might also consider job shadowing with professional event planners.

3. Choose a specialization

If you plan to open your own business, event planners might specialize in one type of event. You can choose to specialize in a specific area, such as weddings, conferences, or business meetings.

4. Obtain a certification

Event planners who have received certifications in event planning may be more attractive to potential employers. The content of certification exams can vary depending on the event planning field. Every certificate has its requirements. However, most require event planners to have completed a training program and had at least five years of experience.

5. Get involved in a professional association

A professional organization can help new event planners make essential connections and expand their career opportunities. You may also find other valuable resources, such as continuing education.

6. Event Planner Job Description

Event planners can gain more job experience and move up the ladder to become program coordinators, meeting directors, or meeting managers. They might also choose to change from a small company to more career opportunities or start their own event planning business.

Event Planner Job Description

Event planners are also known as event specialists or event coordinators. They organize and manage every aspect of events. They are responsible for conceiving theme ideas, planning budgets, and booking venues. They also liaise with clients and suppliers, manage logistics, and present post-event reports.

Event Planner Job Description Template

We are looking for a highly organized, creative event planner to help us create memorable events that increase brand awareness, strengthen business, relationships, and improve employee morale. The event planner will be responsible for creating the ideas, budgeting, communicating with clients and suppliers, and ensuring that every event runs smoothly.

You should be a multitasker and a skilled planner with impeccable attention to detail. You must have an exceptional ability to anticipate and foresee potential risks so that all attendees leave impressed.

Event Planner Responsibilities

- Recognizing the needs and expectations of clients for each event.

- Brainstorming and implementing event themes and concepts.

- Event budget preparation and invoice processing.

- Booking and researching venues.

- Organising caterers, staff, suppliers, and entertainment.

- All logistical aspects of the event should be coordinated.

- Responsible for the management of set-up, tear down, and clean-up operations.

- Preparing for potential risks and anticipating the needs of attendees.

- Develop post-event reports about the event's effectiveness.

Event planner requirements:

- A degree in management, hospitality, public relations, or other related fields.

- Extensive experience in project management and a track record for successful events.

- You have excellent organizational skills and the ability to multitask when under pressure.

- Excellent interpersonal and communication skills.

- Creativity and outside-of-the-box thinking

- Capability to manage a large group and effectively delegate tasks.

- Extreme attention to detail.

- Expert time management skills.

- Financial literacy, including the ability to manage budgets and prepare invoices.

CHAPTER 2

How to Start an Event Planning Service

Do you dream about starting your own event planning company? Maybe you have been in the event and meeting industry for a while and feel that it is now the right time to start your own business. Perhaps you have experience organizing events and think this could be your passion. All of these are good reasons to choose this career. However, anyone contemplating the dream of owning an event planning company must take specific steps before they even start to speak to clients.

Research made us understand that profits in this sector continue to rise. The average profit margin of event planners was just 15 percent a few years back. However, the most recent research shows that profit margins can reach as high as 40%. The industry's health is due to several factors, including the improving economy and corporate America's outsourcing of meeting-planning tasks. Since you're not some tech startup bidding for programmers, you can get started without a lot of money. Let's start with the basics. In general, special events are held for the following reasons:

- Celebrations (festivals, parades, and weddings, as well as reunions, birthdays, and anniversaries)

- Education (conferences and meetings, graduations).

- Promotions (product launches and political rallies, fashion shows, etc.)

- Commemorations (memorials and civic events)

Although this list is not exhaustive, it does illustrate that special events can be business-related, social, or something in between.

24

We now move on to the second question: what is event planning? Event planners may be responsible for any or all of these tasks:

- Research

- Creating an event design

- Locating a site

- Arranging food, decor, and entertainment

- Plan transportation from and to the event

- Invitations sent to the attendees

- Arrange any accommodation for attendees

- Coordination of activities for event personnel

- Supervising the site

- Evaluations of the event

The number of these activities your company engages in will vary depending on the event's size, type, and the specialty you choose.

Why do people hire event planners?

The simple answer to this question is that many people find it difficult or impossible to plan events. These special events can be given the attention they need by independent planners.

Who can become an event planner?

Many planners started in one aspect of planning special events. Martin Van Keken, a business owner, had a successful catering business before he decided to start planning an entire event. Similar stories are shared by many other planners. Planners may not only coordinate events but also provide services.

You may have also started your own event planning business by organizing events for other businesses before you decide to start your own. Joyce Barnes-Wolff worked as an event planner for a retail chain for eleven years before starting her own business.

Becoming a Certified

You might consider getting a certificate or degree from a local university that specializes in event management or planning. Meeting Professionals International (MPI) has a list of universities and colleges that offer education in this area.

Consider pursuing CSEP (Certified Special Events Professional), or CMP (Certified Meeting Planner) certifications. These designations can be obtained by ISES or MPI. These designations are sought by many corporations and the general public when they hire planners. Clients know these planners are professionals because of the amount of research and study required to become a CSEP/CMP.

Target Market

The Corporate Market

There are two types of event planning services available:

social and corporate. Corporate Services can be used to refer to companies, charities, and non-profit organizations. To increase their public support and raise funds, charities and non-profit organizations host gala fundraisers, receptions, and athletic competitions. These events are numerous and you can find small local events that you can start with.

Companies host conventions, trade shows, company picnics, and holiday parties. These types of events are very popular. According to the Convention Industry Council's 2012 Economic Significance Study, 1.83million corporate/business meetings, trade shows, conventions, etc. Only in the U.S.

The Social Market

Weddings, anniversary parties, and Sweet 16 parties are all examples of social events. You can choose to manage all of these events, or you may specialize in one or two.

As baby boomers age, the market for social events will continue to grow, particularly birthdays and anniversaries. These people include children who are getting married, their parents who are celebrating golden anniversaries, and their silver wedding anniversary to remember.

Startup costs

What amount of money do you need to start an event planning business? It will depend on where you live and whether your office is located in a rental or home office. This will also depend on your taste and lifestyle.

Remember that working remotely can help you save money, it is not possible to start a small event planning business.

The following chart shows the startup costs of two possible event-planning companies. The first is a home-based business with no employees. The office space for the high-end business is 1,000 square feet. This business has a full-time manager and a junior planner. Some temporary employees help with clerical work and may be able to prepare for events. Both owners will receive their income from the pre-tax net profits. These businesses will generate an annual income of $85,000 and $250,000 respectively. The startup table shows the pre-opening costs of these businesses.

Startup Expenses	Low	High
Rent	$0	$2,300
Equipment	$5,000	$17,000
Inventory	$0	$500
Licenses and taxes	$250	$350
Communications	$100	$250

Payroll	$0	$4,000
Advertising/Promotion	$500	$2,000
Accounting & Legal Fees	$650	$1,500
Insurance (1st Quarter).	$800	$1,700
Miscellaneous	$750	$1,500
Total	$8,050	$31,100

Operation

Event planners rarely have a 9-to-5 job. Event planning is by its very nature requires you to work nights, weekends, holidays, and sometimes even during specific seasons. The specialization that you choose will determine how much time you have to work.

Social events are more likely to take place on weekends or holidays than corporate events. There are "on" and "off" seasons in some areas and for certain types of events. You can expect to work at least one evening per week, regardless of your specialty (except for parties for young children), as you coordinate and oversee events. However, the planning and execution of these events will take place mostly during business hours.

These are the most important tasks that you will have to complete as an event planner.

Do your research. This is the best way to minimize risk, regardless of type. Research may include conducting focus groups, interviews, and surveys to ensure that there is a demand for large events. Research may be more helpful if you are new to event planning. Talking to other planners who have done events similar to yours is another way to research. You might also find yourself researching customs and etiquette if you are unfamiliar with the event.

Learn event planning skills and experience

Event planning experience is key to the long-term success and longevity of a business. That means, if you're thinking about starting an event planning business, you should have a solid grasp as to what an event planner is, and make sure you have some solid skills:

- Written and verbal communications

- Time and organization

- Budget management and negotiation

- Creativity, marketing, public relations, and more

How to Determine the Event Planning Market/Forte

Let's suppose you have been working in corporate meetings for five years now and want to start your own business. First, you need to recognize that your strengths lie in the corporate world. Many planners make the common mistake of assuming they can coordinate all types of events, such as corporate meetings, fundraising galas, and other special occasions.

You need to stop. Although the desire to offer many services may be strong, your collective past experiences will prepare you. You may eventually be able to handle all types of events. However, you will need to recognize the differences between social, corporate, and association events. Your market should be determined accordingly.

How do you start an event planning business?

When starting an event planning company, there are many things you need to think about. Here are some key points that I found essential when starting my own event planning business.

1. Create a solid business plan

I cannot tell you how many small events planning businesses fail due to the founder not having a business plan.

Start by looking for similar businesses and plans that have been successful in your field of work. Next, reach out to other professionals in the event industry for guidance!

Many online resources and templates will help you get started, even if you have never created a business plan. A current business plan is essential to ensure that you get any investment.

2. If possible, set a marketing budget.

When you start your party planning business, your marketing budget could be as high as 30% of your business expenses. Is that too much? Consider all the things that you will need.

- Website for your business

- Business cards

- Flyers and other printed information

- Online advertising and digital marketing

- Travel expenses to events for networking

Do not leave anything out to make money, you will eventually need to spend money. In the beginning, your goal is to build a customer base quickly. Your clients will continue to recommend you if you live up to your promise of memorable events. Your marketing costs will drop as a result.

3. Define your mission, scope, and goals to run your event business.

While your event planning business will grow over time, it is essential to be clear about what you are and aren't willing to do. This information can be included on your website to attract the right kind of clients.

When you're still building your business, saying "no" to clients is one of the hardest things to do. It can save you time dealing with customers who take too much of your time and don't provide enough value.

4. Prepare your elevator speech.

My 30-second pitch was not well-crafted, and I struggled to sell my first event business. This is what will get everyone to your business.

Tip: Don't worry about the name of your event-planning business. The name of your company doesn't matter if you create memorable events. However, a catchy event business name idea might better stick in someone's brain during an elevator pitch.

5. Do market research

Before you jump, I advise people to research their market and understand their competitors. What is your unique value proposition, what are your fees? Are they similar to, superior to, or higher than those in your local area? This will help you to stand out in the market. This step should not be skipped!

6. Learn tax laws and how to file taxes in your local area.

There are many legal aspects to consider, no matter what type of business you're looking to start. I spent a lot of time researching which type of business would work best for me. The LLC made the most sense for me for my consulting firm. Before you start digging in, it's essential to understand the tax implications fully.

5 Ways to Get Started in Event Planning

There is no one way to plan a great event. This field thrives on creativity, ingenuity, and constant reinvention. There are smart steps you can take to start the journey, learn skills, and establish yourself as a leader in your field.

1. Establish a solid foundation of industry knowledge.

Education is an excellent way to acquire foundational

knowledge about the events industry and the overall hospitality industry. With an industry-specific education foundation, you can stand out from other job candidates. Because you invested in specialized training, you will stand out. This education is as helpful for starting your own event planning business as it is for getting hired. This is a great way to learn about the many planning jobs available in the industry.

Are event planners in high demand

One major thing I kepp telling people is that the events industry is growing--and demand for event planners is expected to grow at a faster-than-average rate of seven percent through 2028.

What degree or certification are you required to become an event planner?

Although you don't have to earn a degree to be an event planner, specific certificates and qualifications can help you stand out.

Numerous colleges and universities offer degree programs in related fields. These courses are taught by industry professionals who understand the business inside and out. You can take either a certificate program or a degree in hospitality. Take advantage of all the networking opportunities they provide.

What skills are required for event planners?

Event planners should be:

- Organized

- Collaboration is encouraged

- Willingness to adapt

- Creativity

- Focused

- Multitasking ability

- Budgeting is a great tool

- An excellent communicator

- Under pressure, composed and calm

- Networking maven

- Are you ready to negotiate?

- Be prepared to travel

Related education for event planners:

- Communications and PR

- Marketing

- Design

- Accounting

- Management

2. All event (and all non-events) experiences can be combined into a relevant experience.

You can build a diverse experience portfolio within the events industry or not. This will show you have a valuable and varied skill set. Are you a food and beverage expert? Your relationship-building skills, food and nutrition knowledge, and multitasking abilities are all strengths. Did you work in retail? You can use your customer insight and people skills to create memorable events that everyone will love. You might be the person who hosts parties for friends and family.

Examine your current jobs and identify your interests in transferable soft skills. Decide how those skills complement the events you want to create and plan, and include them within the experience section of your event planning portfolio.

How to create an event planning portfolio for a new events planner

- *Staged photos of events are a great way to show off your creativity:* Are you a creative and skilled designer of centerpieces? For promotional photos that benefit all parties, connect with local photographers, wedding shops, furniture rental agencies, and models. To showcase your work, take before-and-after photos.

- *Tailor your online presence:* Planners love photo galleries, blog posts, and videos, but they are more about tackling the problem than solving it. *F*ocus on these platforms to get your message across. The goal is not to be everywhere. Superior results are possible with exceptional content.

- To foster online conversations, use your natural abilities as a conversation starter. Share tips, checklists, and your favorite event planning software with other planners, or put together a video travel blog to highlight the best event venues in your area.

- You can start a blog to share your experiences as a

planner. You can network with other planners to offer to write guest blogs for their pages. Check out the submission guidelines for magazines or other publications to get your work in.

- *Don't be afraid to get involved in a cause that is important to you:* Non-profit fundraising is a great way to help charitable organizations. Charity events take the lead or join a committee to gain experience. To gain valuable experience that you can add to your portfolio, take the initiative or join a committee.

- *Collect testimonials from customers:* Ask your professional and personal connections for recommendations, regardless of whether they've ever worked with you or if you have previously planned events. Credibility is enhanced by the right testimonials; this is a clear indication that you are capable of performing as well as you claim.

- *Embrace different portfolio formats:* There is no best portfolio format. There are many options to reach the right clients. Websites allow clients to access your information, while physical portfolios are significant for in-person meetings. Pinterest allows you to gather inspiration and give clients a feel for your style. Potential clients can use your professional Instagram as a social media calling card.

3. You must balance your logistical knowledge with your creative output.

A great event professional can engage both their creative and logical sides in their work.

Successful events are built on logic and logistics. It is essential to be interested in the details and not just the big picture. Event budgets and floor plans will be on your mind. This requires the ability to think logically and plan accordingly. Events that aren't organized or put together with precision can lead to unhappy clients and attendees.

Event planners must think creatively on the other side. This attitude is helpful when you are setting your business aesthetic, designing event themes, and creating graphics. Your creativity makes your event stand out from the rest and gives them that wow (Amoley) factor that attracts clients. A customized event planning checklist can help you manage logistics while ensuring you schedule enough time to generate those big, show-stopping ideas.

Every event planner needs to have access to these free resources:

- Canva: is a graphic design platform that makes creating posters, invitations, flyers, and social media graphics a breeze.

- Grammarly: offers a free grammar checker that

includes tone detection so you can make the best impression when you're reaching out to potential clients.

Keep track of your meetings and appointments with Appointlet, an intuitive scheduling app with a feature-filled free version.

Create your digital portfolio with a website theme from WordPress--free, if you use a 'wordpress.com' branded address, or get even more themes when you connect a wordpress.org account to your hosting and domain name.

4. Start a career as an event planner in the sector that you are passionate about.

You don't have to limit your search when it comes down to looking for events jobs. Many types of organizations hold events and are looking to hire professionals that can take on a planning role. Do you love the work of local non-profits? You can volunteer to be a planner or help design events. If you are interested in healthcare or the arts, associate positions are available at these organizations that will help you build your portfolio.

Whether you're working for a pharmaceutical company and planning their annual convention or working for a small restaurant that plans and hosts social events, you are still gaining valuable experience within events.

At some point in my event career, I had to work for a senior and experienced colleague of mine in event decoration for years without collecting the value of the work that I was working for him then due to the fact that I know what I went there for, and at the end of the day and after successfully finishing each event I went home fulfilled because I gained lots of values. Whatsoever I gained then can never be taken away from me because it's part of my experience, and I can boldly teach people now.

These two acronyms will help you grasp the many opportunities in the events industry.

- **MEEC:** This MEEC stands for "Meetings and Expositions at Events and Conventions" markets. MEEC events are travel, hospitality and corporate events with a business-centric spin.

- **SMERF:** This stands for "Social, Military Educational, Religious, and Fraternal" markets. These markets include weddings, family reunions, and bridal showers. Many SMERF markets include weekend recreational events.

Although planning a weekend trip with transport for 25 people is far from elegant events, it's an excellent way to make connections and learn new things.

5. Establish strong connections in the events sector.

Networking is the best way to jumpstart your career as an event planner. It's all about getting to know others and building relationships. Attend hospitality groups' networking events to get out there. Although networking may seem intimidating at first, it is an essential skill in this field. For event planning success, you need to network in person:

- *Find out how to join a conversation*: It's essential to pay attention to your body language first. Watch out for slightly open-minded people when you approach groups of three or more people in conversation. This signals that they are welcome to join the discussion. Avoid a conversation in which participants are in a closed circle or who have crossed their arms.

- *Start at least one conversation:* Talking about topics is like exercising. The more you do it, the better you will get. Start by practising conversation starters in low-key settings, such as a coffee shop or gym. Then, move on to networking events.

- *Be curious and open-minded*: Networking is more effective when you ask honest questions and share genuine stories about yourself.

- *Remember proper business card etiquette:* Although you should always have your business cards on you, it's not a good idea to just hand your card out because you've had a discussion. It's possible to make connections with people by giving your business card to them. However, passing your card around to everyone you meet is like spamming your email inboxes.

- *Focus on building professional relationships and follow up:* Within 24 hours, follow up. You can remind the person who and whereabouts you met. Also, you can refer to the conversation. Let them know if you found something that resonated with your feelings. You might consider inviting them to coffee if you live close together. Do not ask for

51

favours immediately. Instead, build a relationship and forge a connection. Two-way networking is the best way to network.

Tips for networking online to start your event career:

- *Find out who to contact:* Reaching out to potential clients or event professionals via the internet is a good idea. Make sure you check their profiles on social media and make sure they are open to reaching out. Accept their request if they aren't interested in the solicitation. Don't spam them to project a professional image. Hashtags can be a great tool to network. Keep an eye out for trends and engage when necessary by following your favourite planners.

- *Personalize your outreach:* Emails that are copied and pasted will not work. Do your research. Explore LinkedIn, Twitter, website biographies and other resources to ensure you reach relevant contacts with a message that resonates.

CHAPTER 3

What Makes Event Planning So Stressful?

The event planning job is one of the five most stressful in the world. It follows running into burning buildings or trying to land an eighty-ton aircraft safely. Although planning events seems like a great job, why is it so stressful for so many? It is a job that requires a lot of hard work every day. Communication, budget management, deadlines, working together with third parties, and communication are all things that event planners have to deal with. Let's dive into each category to learn more about how they impact the lives of event planners and what practical approaches can be used to tackle each one.

Communication Challenge: Communication is an essential part of any relationship. In the world of event management, communication skills take on new meanings. Event planners are often messengers between speakers, vendors, guests, staff, and event organizers. It is not easy to organize, communicate and record conversations between different groups. Managers often have to try to communicate with multiple groups through lengthy emails chains that can get confusing. It can also be challenging to track where communication breaks down between emails, texts, Slack, and web calls.

A Simple, Effective Approach: EventOPS is one of the most effective approaches. It provides all-in-one support for event planning and collaboration, as well as security and documentation. We have an amazing way to organize the communication for event planners, from pre-event planning through post-event follow-up. Another option is organization and planning. It's amazing how few Fortune 500 event planners have a "game plan" for their teams. It is a common mistake not clearly to identify who is responsible for what task and establish standards for communication so that it does not get lost or overlapped. This can lead to frustration and stress. Managers will benefit from having a consistent and precise plan. They also need to schedule meetings so that their team can discuss the communication with stakeholders. This will ensure everyone is on the same page and avoid confusing emails.

The Timeline Challenge: Many people find it challenging to meet deadlines. More than 25% of people admit to being chronic procrastinators. With thousands of speakers and attendees, a large budget means that every minute is essential and tasks must be completed efficiently. Event planners are bound to meet their deadlines. This may mean working 12 hours a day, eating only light meals, and sleeping little. Event planners who fail to meet their deadlines could ruin the event.

A Simple, Effective Approach: It is possible to resolve

deadline problems by returning to communication's original challenge. Even though event managers are often expected to plan and execute every detail of an event, organizing employees, guests, and third parties can make even simple events complicated. Event planners should ask their team for assistance and recognize that they are not the only ones trying to meet deadlines. Event OPS makes it easy to organize your deadlines and sync your calendar to know exactly what you need to do on each day at all your events.

The Budget Challenge: A large percentage of people find money to be one of their most stressful aspects. Budgeting money can be difficult and stressful. It's not surprising that managing an entire event within a limited budget can be stressful and have different opinions on how the budget should go. Last-minute issues and the need for additional expense add to this stress.

A Simple, Effective Approach: EventOPS' budget

organization system updates your budget as you add more information throughout the event. For all events, a clear budget must be prepared with supporting details and a high-level view. Then the expense should be measured. This is a good way for management to report on the actual ROI of events and areas where cost savings can be made without compromising the event's goals. It is essential to organize spreadsheets efficiently to keep track of event planners' budgets. To ensure that all information is accurate, you must always use the most up-to-date and precise spreadsheet. This can be achieved by allowing one or two people to edit the spreadsheet. Then, they will continue to work on the latest version and delete any previous versions. To ensure that the spreadsheet is being shared with only you, you should allow others to comment and not to edit it.

CHAPTER 4

8 Event Planning Jobs for Aspiring Events Professional

Event management requires many skills. These include the ability to plan and execute events well, as well as multitasking. Some people are not able to see the big picture or solve problems in chaos.

If you believe you are a professional event planner, Check out these options, event planning jobs might be right for you.

1. Conferences and galas are all possible event planners do it all.

This is why this role is ideal for multitaskers. Planners organize all logistics, including food, decor, staff, presenters, and technology, to ensure a flawless event.

They may even manage large-scale events such as trade shows or coordinate complicated conference schedules for thousands.

Do you want to be the person people go to? Planners are responsible for solving any unforeseen problems or obstacles that may arise during the event's execution. Although it can be a stressful job, the satisfaction of completing a successful event is priceless.

2. The wedding industry is a big one.

They turn to the experts when couples want to ensure their big day runs smoothly.Wedding planners. These professionals are in the industry learn the intricacies of each wedding topic from cakes and dresses to sound systems and marriage certificates.

They assist their clients in making decisions that meet their needs and fit their budgets during the planning phase. They help relieve the couple of the stress that comes with the big day. They help to make sure that the couple can enjoy their wedding day without having to worry about any issues or decisions.

3. Event Space Managers

Managers of event space and venues are experts in their space. They are experts in how to put on a great event within their own space. It doesn't matter if it's an arena or a concert hall. They know how to arrange logistics and create ambiance. You can find many different events.

Many venue managers also serve as the marketing and sales managers for the space. They help promote and bring in new events. Sometimes they can also serve as event planners or assist the event planner in executing the perfect event.

4. Many charities rely on donations to continue their operations.

Donor coordinators help raise these funds by hosting

lunches, dinners, and other fundraising events. This is a great way to thank donors for their support.

These professionals often cater to the needs and interests of well-off businesspeople and community leaders. They are skilled at catering to the needs of guests.

That's why a donor or sponsorship coordinator needs exceptional people skills, tenacity, and the ability to create meaningful relationships with sponsors.

5. Catering Services Manager

Are you passionate about food? You might be a catering manager. Your job may require you to cook for hundreds or create a five-course dinner for a small group. It is vital. You must keep clients and guests happy.

Catering managers must have a background in food preparation and innate or formal skills in problem-solving and planning.

6. Event Social Media Coordinator

Social Media has had a profound impact on every industry. But perhaps most importantly, it has had a significant impact on the events industry. Social Media Coordinators are responsible for coordinating social media. Promote events via social media to gain exposure for the event. They might create hashtags unique to their event, host live streams, or design digital advertising campaigns.

The event's success is dependent on the efforts of social media coordinators. They are also crucial during event execution to show the event live. It will also allow you to interact with technology in event planning.

7. Many events are dependent on volunteers or temporary help to succeed.

A staff coordinator is saddled with responsibility related to the personnel present at the event.

Warning: It can be difficult to train large numbers of

employees and increase productivity quickly. This is especially true if your staff has less stake in the success of the event.

Volunteers and temporary staff often lack the necessary knowledge to understand the inner workings of an event. They are unable to be proactive when there are problems. The volunteer coordinator must be able to think quickly and find solutions to unexpected situations.

It could be a great job if you enjoy working with many different people.

8. You might be a mid-sized company's marketing or communications manager: Responsible for coordinating promotional events and other experiential marketing. Your team will most likely help you with event marketing.

You can have both marketing and events, so it's possible to get the best of both. This can spice up your workload and allow you to see your promotions in action.

CHAPTER 5

7 Key Elements of Event Management

Without the input of the six key elements that make up events, such as event infrastructure, clientele, organizers, venue, media, and clients, no event can succeed. Exhibits also demonstrate that there is no difference between national and international events at the conceptual level. The factors that make an event different are almost entirely dependent on the socioeconomic and technological conditions in the area.

The event hexagon is a graphic representation of how event organizers plan and execute every activity related to an event. Event infrastructure can be defined as the combination of the core concepts, people, and talent.

The event's ultimate experience is for the target audience. This is why the event organizer carefully designs it. From the perspective of event organizers, the client is the financier or sponsor of an event venture.

Media is the medium that communicates details about the event to the target audience. The venue is the place where the event will be held.

1. Event infrastructure : As the name suggests, all of the essential elements that are required to make an event a success. These fundamental elements include core concept, core people, and core talent. This infrastructure's nature varies depending on the event category and the variations in events.

2. A core concept: is a term used to describe the fundamental ethos and evolution for the major categories of events. This is what distinguishes and delimitates the boundaries among the different categories.

The core concept of an event can be compared to a root that is planted under a tree. It generates energy and provides the foundation for the type of tree that will grow.

Trees of the same family may vary in size and shape. Each event category can be used to create an entire family.

3. Major People: These are the people who perform, act, or participate in the influence process to make a positive impression on the audience and create a favorable image for clients' brands in their minds. These are the people who control the stage and take center stage when the event begins.

They are there to share their knowledge, expertise, and charisma with the audience. The brand personality should reflect the nature of the core team members who will be participating in the event.

4. Major Talent: Each event requires that the core team have specific knowledge, expertise, and reputation. The

core talent is what attracts and inspires the audience. The skill of the performer will determine the type of audience at a concert.

The core talent is what gives room for the creation of variations in every event category. It doesn't matter if the event is classical or pop; it all depends on what type of music is being played.

Similar to sports, every game has limited time and constraints. These physical constraints can be a challenge or an obstacle in different games, which means that each game requires different skills.

One example is that in sports competitions, the core talent required is game-specific. The talent required for cricket is different from that needed to play basketball.

5. Major Structure: It is crucial to have a formal or informal organization that manages the entire event category to make it profitable from a marketing

standpoint.

The requirements for managing and marketing events will vary depending on how structured an event is. It is more profitable to market an event category that is more structured.

We mean more structured and formal. This means that there is an organizational structure where roles and responsibilities are clearly delegated to the appropriate members of the organization.

Each category has been structured in a different way, depending on the stakes. The core structure is an organization that allows for efficient management.

The traditional approach to competitive events has been to start at the grassroots level. From the school level all the way to the international level.

In fact, only competitive events have an organized and strong organization. Sporting events are among the most organized and structured national and international events.

Examples of such sports control bodies are the BCCI (Board of Control for Cricket in India) and the ICC (International Cricket Council).

These bodies are responsible for managing the event and ensuring that players receive the benefits of the event.

6. Target Audience: The customer segments that are the focal point of events are called the target audience. The event design depends on the demographic profile and the number of targeted audiences.

These criteria are what determine the event's image and budget. It is essential to consider whether the event will be a mega-event, theme party or if the artist performing at the event will be there. The target audience is the most essential factor.

From the initial concept to the execution of the event, the

whole process takes into account the behavior and characteristics of target customers.

Customer-based marketing activities are the basis of every marketing activity. Event organizers choose the target audience based on their marketing needs, as we discussed earlier.

The event organizer can use the target audience as a common factor to find other clients interested in the event. Events can be used as a platform for diverse corporates with similar target audiences. Costing for an event will depend on the audience and profile.

Understanding the potential differences in event design that may arise from a change of target audience profile can help you understand the importance of the target audience.

This transformation from Rang Barse and Holi Gyrations is an excellent example of how event design varies depending on the audience.

The title was changed from its original ethnic and traditional tone to make it more appealing to a large group of young people.

The event's target audience profile has an impact on how the audience will perceive it. However, the audience size also plays a significant role in the design. Because the expected audience is the key determinant of venue cost and other associated costs, this is why the venue and related costs are determined.

The event design can suffer if the target audience is not the same. To design successful events, it is not enough to consider the audience profile.

7. Clients: are people or companies that act as sponsors for any event. Sponsors sponsor events because they see them as an effective marketing tool that allows them to position themselves in the minds and hearts of their target

audience.

They either partially or fully subsidize an event to make it more affordable for its target audience. The risk rating of an event rises if sponsors don't provide enough funds to support it.

Corporate clients may be event-savvy, or they might need to be educated on the benefits and uses of events as a strategic communication tool. Event-savvy companies look for greater value from event organizers.

Clients must be actively involved in the event activities to get more value. Clients must be involved in every aspect of the event, from its planning to execution. One thing I always tell my clients is that, no matter how skilled the event organizer is, the client must also be prepared and participate in the event effectively.

CHAPTER 6

Event Planner Fee Structure

Whether you're starting an event planning business for social events, business events, or a combination of both, you should know how to charge for services.

Several factors go into determining your rate, including event planning and operating expenses, salaries, and profits. Rates will vary depending on the location of your business, the type of projects you take on, and what the market is willing or able to pay.

How event planners structure their fees

If you want to start a part-time or even full-time business, there are roughly five ways to structure your event fee and quote your fees to your clients:

- Flat project fee

- Percentage of expenses

- Hourly rate

- Percentage of expenses and an hourly rate

- Rates for commission

Let's say you are looking to make an average of $75 an hour for your services.

Fees based on a flat project rate

Many clients want to know the total cost of a project, including all fees.

Flat project fees are usually used for packaged events such as those associated with sports marketing programs. They may be charged per person with many conditions and caveats. The client can contract directly with an event planner to handle all logistics, catering, venue, lodging, and other expenses.

Let's say, for example, that you are hired to lead a tour of a historic city for 15 people. The client asks you to provide a flat fee, including transportation, a private guide, lunch, and all admission fees to the venues. They also request that you give a detailed breakdown of each expense item.

As an event planner, to offer this, you must come up with a flat fee by determining how much all aspects of the project will cost. Negotiate and determine the total cost of all services.

You are responsible for managing your budget and must anticipate possible changes. You are responsible for identifying required deposits and paying for all services.

Fees based on a percentage of expenses

Event planners will typically charge between 15% and 20% of the event's total cost as part of their fees. It all depends on how complex the event is and how long it takes to plan and execute. Sometimes, this amount will be enough to cover the entire cost of an event planner and their source of profit.

Let's say you're being hired to host a private dinner at a prestigious restaurant for 40 people. The average cost per head is $175. It will take approximately 15 hours to meet your client, plan, organize, and follow up on the event. You will make just $75 per hour if you charge 18% of your total expenses.

$175 x 40 guests = $7,000 + 18% = $1.260

15 hours x 75/hr = $1.125

If the client contracts directly with you, the total event expense cost would amount to $8,260.

Hourly Rate Fees

Clients may prefer that the event planner quotes an hourly rate and estimates the time to manage and execute a client program. Although it may look similar to a flat project rate, it allows both parties more flexibility to adapt to any changes.

Many event planners charge hourly. This allows clients to see how much it will cost for your services and to help them calculate a budget. Clients want to be able to plan for unexpected costs.

Be sure to set clear expectations to ensure that everyone is on the same page about what services they will receive. You should also include billing information for any reasonable business expenses you may incur as an event planner.

Event planners might mark up expenses like shipping and car rental as high as 15-20%. You should inform your client about such markups in advance and get their consent.

It is essential to establish how often you will bill for your hourly event planning rate.

For example, let's assume that a client is hiring you in October to organize a one-day seminar in March. Your services are being contracted to source and negotiate for the venue, catering services, and contribute to the content creation for a limited number of communications items (i.e., invitations, schedule, evaluation forms, etc.

You will also be providing on-site management services for your client. An agreement is made upfront that you will invoice for the services identified at different times and submit invoices detailing all services rendered on a weekly or biweekly basis.

You and your client must agree on a detailed work statement that includes both the expected responsibilities. You can then estimate the total cost of your work, including reasonable expenses. Be clear about what these details might include.

Fees based on Percentage of Expenses plus Flat

Fee/Hourly

Sometimes, you are hired to organize an event. For whatever reason, the client prefers a flat rate that is based on a percentage. This is not enough to cover your time and costs. It is acceptable to present your fees in two categories.

A client might hire you to help organize events for a conference. You are assigned to host two private dinners with 50 guests and a golf tournament. These events will cost approximately $20,000 but require 60 hours of your time. The complexity of the project could justify a higher profit margin. Keep this in mind when calculating your final flat fee or hourly rate.

Estimated Percentage of Expenses:

$20,000 x 18% = 3,600

Hourly Rate Estimate:

60 hours x $75/hr = 4,500

Hourly Deficit

$3,600-$4,500 = $900

You may need to estimate 15 hours for logistics management if you run into a shortfall, such as in the above example. The following may be included in your quote:

Subtotal Event Expenses $23,600

Flat Fee $1,125 based on 15 hours of $75/hr

This scenario will require you to ensure that your hours are accurately estimated (an account to cover non-standard operating costs such as travel). Few clients like to see expenses rise later unless there are justifiable reasons.

Based on commissionable rates, fees

Event planners can also collect fees by booking event space through venues that have a commissionable rate. These fees are typically charged to travel agents when booking tickets, hotel rooms, or other forms of transportation.

For example, many hotels may extend a commissionable rate up to 10% for guest rooms and other expenses.

While some event planners may accept commissionable rates as an income source, more sophisticated clients might question their loyalty when there are commissionable rates. Many seasoned planners will not accept commissionable rates or negotiate pricing that is non-commissionable for their programs. They pass the savings to their clients.

Some clients might not know commissionable rates and may not expect outside consultants to bill them using the identified billing methods. However, they will still have to pay a commissionable fee. Many event planners don't think it's a good idea to "double-dip" their revenue streams in this manner.

Accepting commissioned rates is a good idea. It's better not to charge client fees using other billing methods.

In some cases, commissionable rates are the best option. For example, a smaller nonprofit organization or association may hire your services for a meeting or membership event. Attendees and not the organization pay the bulk of the fees.

You may also be able to offer promotional item distribution services if you are selling client gifts. If this is the case, you can negotiate for promotional items and don't charge an hourly rate unless your client knows all details upfront.

CHAPTER 7

10 Tips to Be a Better Event Planning Consultant

Events are like works of artwork for you: Each event starts with a vision. You carefully plan how you will get there. The vision becomes a reality step by step. Your event will become more tangible with time, effort, and some struggle.

No matter how good your event planning skills are, there's always more you can do for your clients and the events that you plan. This is why I and my team created this list of tips to help you become a better event planner. These best practices will make your next event unforgettable.

1. Keep your mind open

You will develop your style of planning as you move up the ladder in your career. It's essential to be open to the suggestions of your team members, clients, or event volunteers.

Problem-solving should be done in collaboration, even if they have less experience than you. It will improve the event overall, but will also give critical participants a sense of belonging.

2. Choose the proper organization method for yourself

Let's face facts; it's unlikely that you will be able to memorize or recall all of the information required to plan your event. Use tools and resources to help you plan. Selecting world-class event management software will help you plan better events in less time. In addition, you might want to consider incorporating some task management tools into your workday to help you keep track of key deliverables.

3. Social media is your chance to stand out

LinkedIn. Twitter. Facebook. Pinterest. Tumblr. You need to keep up with them all to build your brand and attract clients.

Create Pinterest boards to build your network. Pinterest allows users to pin things that they find interesting. This is your chance to show off your personality and goals for your company. Pin content that is interesting and relevant to your followers to expand your network. Keep search engines in your mind when you create descriptions for both your pins and boards.

Utilize Facebook to market directly to potential clients. Many professionals have a Facebook page that they regularly check. This is a great way to reach people in need of your services. Post content that is engaging, well-designed, and not too flashy to promote your business. You will be a thought leader within the planning industry if you share valuable content on Facebook.

Finally, connect to like-minded professionals using LinkedIn. LinkedIn offers a lot of great features that will help you connect with potential clients. For example, LinkedIn Communities allow users to share content with others in the same industry. LinkedIn Pulse is another great tool. It enables you to access content from industry leaders and allows LinkedIn users to share original content with their connections.

4. Create lasting connections

Your clients will still be a driving force for the event's success, even though you are in charge of most work. It will help you to position yourself as someone interested in assisting clients to achieve success by researching your clients.

Set up Google Alerts to notify your client about the top competitors and their companies. This will allow you to stay in the loop while you work with your client's company. To show that you care about their best interests, you might even email clients information you find on competitors.

Your clients will appreciate your efforts to work with them. You can mention their names in emails, newsletters, and social media posts even after the event is over.

Ask your clients if they would be willing to refer you after a successful event. You will be able to find and convert new clients quicker if you use positive experiences from past clients to show how good a planner you are.

As a way to win new business, you might also consider asking clients to be referenced. To make it easy to share customer testimonials, create a single document that contains all your customer testimonials.

5. Read event planning blogs

Look to the words of others when all else fails. Blogs are a great way to learn from other event planners and businesses.

6. Keep your team informed

Communication is the key to building a team that succeeds. To ensure that an event runs smoothly, you and your team need to be on the same page.

You can keep everyone up-to-date by asking your team for a daily progress report. This will include information about what they have accomplished and what is still needed later in the week.

To make communication between teams easier, you can create a group chat using apps such as GroupMe or WhatsApp or Telegram.

7. Figuring out how to hire and train event

talent is crucial.

Your job will be easier if you can attract millennial candidates. They are the largest age group to be employed.

Inc. reports that members of Generation Y are more likely to be "disconnected from institutions but close to friends." If you make your company seem too personal, they will be disinterested in working with you as clients or employees.

Instead of portraying your company's institution as something you do, show it as a group that is passionate about creating unforgettable experiences.

It's not all about the money; it's about the fulfillment. Numerous psychological studies have shown that people, not just Millennials, are happier when they spend their money on living rather than having.

If you create an event planning company focused on

creating great experiences for clients and attendees, it will be easier to attract more clients and better talent.

8. Create interactive events

Today's audience is short-attention-span. Speakers often struggle to hold their attention, and many people have trouble with distractions. Engage your audience by making it fun and interactive for them to absorb information.

A growing trend among event planners is to use either virtual or augmented reality during events. You can submerge your attendees into a new world or enhance the one already in place. The Consumer Electronics Show had a pavilion dedicated to virtual and augmented realities. This allowed visitors to wear headsets and see a simulation of life as a Fashion Week model.

In the next few years, interactive elements in live events

will be more popular. These new technologies will soon be a boon for event organizers who can master them now.

Virtual and augmented reality are just two of the many anticipated trends for conference and event technology that will be more prevalent at successful conferences and events.

9. Make an event emergency kit

Sometimes things can go wrong, even with all the planning. It could be a bad cable or a malfunctioning Wifi. These minor mishaps shouldn't be a problem. To avoid disaster, make sure you have these tools in your emergency kit.

- Ethernet cables (in case wifi goes down)

- USB Drives

- Extension cords and power strip

- Display cables (HDMI and VGA cables).

- Mini display cable converters (for Apple computers)

Contact information for people responsible for:

- event planning software

- Venue staff

- A/V staff

- Catering

- Duct tape and glue dots

- Chargers for your phone and laptop

These little items can save your life when you are in a tight spot. They may even make you the event hero! These small items will save you!

10. Follow up with clients/team members

Once the event is over, be sure to thank everyone who contributed their time and effort. Recognize the people who helped you coordinate the event, whether it be through thank-you notes or newsletters.

To find out how your event planning consultants can improve, you could send your clients a satisfaction questionnaire. Free survey tools like Typeform are a great inexpensive way to collect and analyze feedback from your clients.

NOTE: There are many options, types of consulting. Sometimes, lessons from these fields can be applied to events. In other cases, there are lessons that only event consulting can teach.

Be a better communicator, more open-minded leader, and a more efficient messenger by keeping your team informed. You can be prepared for any situation by keeping an emergency kit with you. You can stay on top of your game with a task management tool and some favorite event planning blogs. Social media is a great way to expand your professional horizons. You can take your business relationships to the next level by building trust and goodwill with clients. This will help you appeal to new clients and employees. Virtual reality is a great way to engage your guests. You can also ask for feedback from clients to help you improve the skills and knowledge you already have.

10 Tips To Successfully Manage An Event

Event organizers can feel overwhelmed when planning an event. Our top 10 tips for Successful Event Management will help you to master the fine art of planning a memorable and effective event.

1. Start Early

Plan as soon as possible. You should plan your event at least four to six months ahead of time if it is a large one. For smaller events, it is best to plan at least one month in advance. You can keep the event running smoothly by ensuring that vendor contracts are in place at least a few weeks prior to the event.

2. Keep it Flexible

Things will change as you plan the event. You need to be flexible and able to meet changing needs, regardless of the event location or event time.

3. Negotiate

Contrary to what vendors may tell you, all prices are negotiable. Keep in mind that every event will have unexpected costs so make sure to negotiate a low price. Before meeting with vendors, determine your budget and offer to pay 5-10% less than that figure. Although your vendor might try to fight you, ultimately they want your business.

4. Assign Responsibilities

You can break down the different elements of the event into separate sections (e.g. Each member of your team should be assigned a section. They will be more knowledgeable about small details as they are responsible for their section.

5. Make a shared document

Cloud computing offers many advantages, making it easier to collaborate with your team. To keep everyone on the same page and ensure that everything is in order, create a central manual. This document will include information about vendor contracts, attendees, and the floor plan. Everyone can refer to the shared document if they have any questions. The entire team can also spot any mistakes.

6. Make sure you have a backup plan

Rarely is an event successful without at least one problem. An item might not arrive on time or someone may be late. Make a list of the most valuable assets that your event has and make a backup plan. You can triage any future issues and determine if an alternative solution is possible or should the event be canceled entirely.

7. Do a Run Through

Do a walkthrough of the entire event process two weeks prior to the event. You can organize a meeting with your team to mentally go through the entire event, from set-up to follow-up. These meetings are a great way to highlight any problems and give you the chance to fix them. You can also arrange another run-through at the venue a few days before the event.

8. Take pictures of everything

Positive photos are a great way to show the success of an event. A professional photographer is more likely to have the right information and will contact you for details. To ensure that you have all the bases covered, ask for several shots, including photos of the entire room, branding photos, and photos of attendees having fun.

9. Social Media

A social media event is a great way to increase your presence. Use a hashtag to promote your event on Twitter, and encourage followers to share it. Create a Facebook event and ask your followers to tag it in the appropriate posts. Once the event is over, upload your photos and encourage others to tag you.

10. Follow up immediately.

Many event organizers make the common mistake of taking a vacation after the event has ended. It is possible to organize logistics, but it is crucial to follow up with attendees via email or social media to show the event's success.

CHAPTER 8

What Events Should You Focus Your Attention On Right Now

When planning an event, there are many things that event planners must consider. Let's get back to basics. It is essential to determine the type of function that you would like to host. Virtual and hybrid events are becoming increasingly popular. Many types of live events can also be done online. What are some other ideas for event ideas? Here's a list of the most popular categories: virtual, corporate, fundraisers, festivals.

Corporate events

It is common to hear the term "corporate events" all the time. But what does it mean? Put simply, a corporate event is an activity that's organized by a business and is intended for employees, clients, stakeholders, a charity, or the public. The purpose of the event will determine the audience. It might be to launch a new product, celebrate staff achievements, or demonstrate expertise in a particular field. Some corporate events are held every quarter or year, while others may be held once a year to announce a significant event or award.

- **Seminars:** Seminars are designed to reach a targeted audience and provide relevant information. You can host this type of event in a community space or at your company headquarters. Or, you can even do it online through a platform such as a Zoom or Vimeo. It's typical for a single speaker or a small number of speakers, to address the audience, so researching speakers and approaching potential sponsors should be high on your seminar planning checklist.

- **Conferences:** are more complicated events that feature multiple speakers and sessions in a variety of venues. Conferences are a great way to encourage conversations and give people a platform for sharing their expertise. They are also one of the most successful types of business networking events. Usually, they start with a keynote session and then move on to interviews, roundtables and panel discussions.

- **Shows for trade:** Trade shows are a great way to show off your product and introduce your brand to other businesses and the public. Trade shows are usually held in large venues that allow many vendors. Trade shows are a great way to generate leads and sales.

- **Workshops:** Many business-to-business events (B2B) will fall under one of these three categories. However, workshops and training sessions can be an excellent way for businesses to connect with staff and the general public. These corporate events can be used to bring people together to brainstorm ideas or to help them understand your product better.

Social events

There are many reasons to gather a group of people away from work or the workplace, such as an anniversary celebration or team-building event. Social events should reflect the interests of individuals and revolve around entertainment and eating.

- **Reunions:** Reunions can be anything from a reunion with old classmates to a celebration of an important anniversary. You can have speeches, music played by a DJ, or a slide show of old photos. The event should encourage people to reminisce. The best way to capture the memories made is by hiring a videographer and photographer. If invitees live in different countries, you can make your reunion virtual to allow everyone to attend.

- **Event Creator:** A great event creator will always find an excuse to celebrate, and hosting a themed party can help make decisions around the types of event marketing, decorating, and catering that you opt for. A creative idea can be timeless, whether it is for intimate gatherings or more significant online events.

Virtual Events

Virtual events take place online, where attendees can join in from the comfort of their own homes. A growing (and necessary) event type in recent times, online events are here to stay as an ideal way to boost your business. Online events offer the opportunity to reach a wider audience because geographic boundaries do not limit you. Online events offer several budget-friendly benefits, such as the ability to rent or cater for venues and fewer restrictions regarding physical accessibility.

1. Webinars: A webinar is an online presentation that addresses a topic to a virtual audience. It can be either academic, such as a historical event, business-focused, or sales masterclass. There is usually enough time to have a Q&A at the end. This format is especially well-suited for educational talks because there is usually only one presenter at any given time. There are plenty of great platforms for running a webinar, including Vimeo and YouTube.

2. Classes: Many online classes cover everything, from twerking to wine-tasting. Extra points to consider for a virtual class are whether you need to send out samples (for food or drink tastings) if your students need any special tools (for a cooking or pottery class), and how well your technology works. You might need to purchase better-quality audio equipment so attendees can hear you.

3. Interactive performances: Performers who are entrepreneurial have discovered new ways to perform or plays other live performances. Online comedy gigs are possible. VIP tickets allow people to pay extra to access the virtual audience and be "picked up" by the host. Everyone else can watch the live stream in safety. Another successful event type is a virtual murder mystery, with creators offering online challenges and the audience helping to solve the crime.

4. Summits: This type of collaborative event is very similar to an in-person conference, but it takes place online. The tickets give attendees access to many talks, interviews, presentations and other activities following a common theme. You will also find interactive elements such as "breakout rooms" that allow for mastermind sessions or networking.

Fundraising events

As the name suggests, the goal for these events is to generate funding for an organisation. It's not surprising that non-profits and schools sports clubs often use these events.

- Items that are sold at a higher price during fundraising bidding wars may be more profitable for charities. A catalogue of items is helpful to give people time to choose what they want to bid on. They will be more inclined to place a higher bid if they are attached to the item. Online or in-person auctions are possible. You could auction off classic items such as artworks or services like personal training sessions, dinner at a well-respected restaurant, and so on.

- Another way to raise money is to challenge your friends and family by asking them for sponsorship money. Examples of events include relay races, long-distance walks, and triathlons - and in recent years, obstacle courses like Tough Mudder and Iron Man have gained popularity. Virtual runs are also becoming more common, as they're easier to organise. People can run the race at their own pace using trackers to keep them updated.

- Sales: A stall selling baked goods, seedlings is a proven method of fundraising. It can be transformed into a community event by allowing others to set up a booth in return for a pitch fee or a monetary donation.

- Gala dinners: These glamorous events often include entertainment and a fancy dinner. The attendees pay the cost of a table. They are also encouraged to donate generously through a raffle, auction, or other competition. It's worth asking suppliers to sponsor these events by waiving or reducing their fees in return for the chance to support a worthy cause.

Festivals

A festival can be described as an organized series of performances or events with the same theme, such as music, food or comedy. You can have it in one place, like a park or field, or spread out over multiple venues within a city. Festivals usually last for one day or more, while some span a whole month, so you'll need to be extra prepared.

- It's a good idea to hire acts from similar genres to host a music festival. This will help you target your audience and narrow down your audience. For variety, you might also consider hiring comedians or other acts. Virtual music events are usually more affordable than in-person ones. You can either pre-record your performance and stream it live on the day, or you can do it via Facebook or Zoom. There are also immersive platforms like Sansar to give attendees a more realistic festival experience.

- Food festivals include food trucks, live demonstrations, food vendors, and tents selling foodie goods like the latest ingredients or kitchen tools. These festivals are great for bringing people together. A virtual food festival can be held by asking people to pay for personalized meal boxes, which are delivered directly to their doorstep. You can also use a video hosting platform to host meal and vendor chats.

Community Events

Community events are designed to bring people together, create positive change, and build relationships between people in your town or neighbourhood.

- *Street parties:* A street party is a great way to bring your neighbours together, regardless of whether it's

111

a long-table setup or a door-to-door drink situation. This is often done for special events like the Royal Jubilees. There are rules and regulations that you must follow. To request a road closure, you will always need to contact your local council.

- *Swap shops:* Host a swap shop in your neighbourhood for second-hand items. This is a fun way to meet people and reduce waste. Everyone sets up a table or stall and then fills it with items they don't need anymore. There is no need to pay anything for the items you take, and leftovers can be donated to local charities.

- *Litter-picking and many other things:* There is nothing that says "community" better than getting together to improve your environment. You can organize a day of volunteer work to improve your community's environment. This could include picking up litter, raking leaves or guerrilla gardening. It's also possible to knock on doors and offer assistance to elderly neighbours with their gardening or weeding.

Hybrid Events

Hybrid events are a fantastic option in the current climate, where some attendees are itching to return to live events, and others may still feel apprehensive. This type of event includes both virtual and in-person elements. This is where the key to success lies in meeting the needs of every kind of attendee. To make virtual guests feel more like they are at the event, you can send them food and drink samples. You could also allow them to purchase merchandise on the day. These are just a few examples of hybrid events.

- *Festivals:* Maybe you organize live music performances that can be streamed to your fans around the globe. Perhaps it's a festival of film that highlights new talent through series of screenings. These can be viewed in person at the event or online. If your budget can stretch to it, creating an immersive virtual venue can make online attendees feel like they're really at the festival.

- *Conference:* Some conference organizers hosted hybrid events even before the pandemic. Events that bring together industry leaders to share their knowledge can be held at a conference centre and live-streamed to remote attendees. This allows you to reach a larger audience and increases the capacity of your event. Incorporate interactive tools such as chat boxes and breakout rooms in Q&As or networking sessions to ensure that everyone can enjoy the social side of your event.

Pop-up events

Pop-ups are a must for any event list. Pop-ups are a temporary event that only lasts for a limited time. Pop-ups can be held for just one night or a whole month. Examples of pop-up events include foodies who want to increase their reach by opening a temporary restaurant or a business that generates excitement before a full launch.

1. *Boutique shops:* Pop-up shops are more successful when they have a common theme, such as celebrating local vendors, vintage fashion or current homeware trends. Remember that you have limited time to sell all your products when you are sourcing them. Another way to host a pop-up shop is to organise it like a market and have the artists host their stalls themselves to interact directly with attendees.

2. *Food collaborations:* You can add some flavour to your local food scene by partnering with a well-known restaurant to create a unique take-out

experience. Working with other respected businesses will allow you to cross-market and possibly attract loyal customers. To create an exclusive feeling, ask people to send you a direct message asking for a delivery slot and a menu.

3. *Exercise classes:* Personal trainers can gauge whether they would be interested in long-term contracts by renting studio space and offering courses for a limited time. This is a great way to establish yourself as an instructor.

Making a profit in the Event Planning Business

The Entrepreneur Media Inc. staff and Cheryl Kimball, writer, explain how to get started in event planning, no matter if you are looking forward to plan a wedding, birthday party, or bar mitzvah, or work part-time. They also discuss product launches and political fundraisers. The authors provide an edited excerpt that explains how to decide what event planning clients should be charged.

Your business's success depends on your ability to charge enough, but not too much, for event planning services. First-time business owners should be cautious when estimating the event's cost. Pricing a service should be done in a way that allows you to charge overhead costs and still make a profit.

According to Dr. Joe Goldblatt, fees are usually determined by three factors.

- *Market segment served:* Corporate events are charged differently from social events. Planners in the social events sector typically charge a fee and a percentage of any or all vendor fees. According to Patty Sachs, an industry expert, social planners would make between $12 and $75 an hour if you broke down the event planning fee into hourly charges. Vendor commissions are also included. Planners in the corporate events sector typically charge a fee and a handling fee for each item. A planner might buy flowers from a florist and mark them up (15% usually) before charging the client that amount. A flat fee or "project fee" is another option. This is often used for large events where the company wants a "not-to-exceed" amount. Sachs estimates that a corporate planner's hourly rate is $16 to $150 plus vendor commissions.

- *Geographic location:* for example, fees are more expensive in the Northeast than they are in the Southeast. This is due to the differences in living costs. Additionally, prices in areas with clearly defined on- and offseasons (e.g. the Hamptons in New York, Martha's Vineyard in Massachusetts) are based partly on the season.

- *The event planner's reputation and experience:* It's okay to charge less if you are just getting started in the industry. However, you should not demand too much just to get the job. Clients may shop around to find the best price. However, a planner that offers too low a quote could be just as annoying as one that charges too much. Based on what you've quoted, your client might question your ability or willingness to host a high-quality event.

How are the fees-for-service mentioned above calculated? Event planners use a cost-plus method to price their service fees (the total cost to clients). Event planners contract out labour, supplies, and materials and charge their clients between 10 and 20% of the total event cost. A rough estimate is 15%.

Before you plan an event, it is important to understand what your clients want and their budget. Next, estimate

119

the cost of labour and supplies. Add your commission to this and then present an estimate to the client. Here are some examples of per-event costs:

Site rental: Site rental fees vary depending on the event. They can be high, low, or indifferent. You have the opportunity to save money on behalf of clients who are tight on budget. Maybe a client is looking for a beautiful summer barbecue. While a site on a public beach is often available for virtually nothing, well-respected beachside clubs can command high prices.

Vendors: This could include, a caterer/bartender, decorator/florist, photographer, videographer, or entertainer.

Stock: Your company will have to purchase any supplies that the vendor or client does not provide. You can buy anything, from food and potted trees to table lamps.

Equipment rental: It is possible to rent audiovisual and lighting equipment.

Permits and licenses: Certain types of events may require licenses or permits that are not available to everyone, such as a permit for a fire marshal or a license to perform a musical score.

Transport and parking: There may be significant transportation, expenses if you or your staff travel for the event or provide transport for speakers or attendees.

Gratuities and service fees: Temporary help, such as servers, can be expensive.

Speakers' fees: Speakers are often a part of conferences and other commemorative or educational events.

Invitations and publicity: Fliers may be required for smaller events as well as large-scale events. Invitations are often required.

Shipping and mail: Don't forget to include this cost if you send out flyers or invitations. Some event planners even ship flowers.

Photocopying and preparation for registration materials: This category includes handouts to attendees and photocopying of flyers.

Signage: All signs and banners that are used for the event must be included in your per-event costs.

Once you have a list of all the expenses, you can calculate the event cost and fee-for-service. Start by getting three vendors and suppliers to find out the current rate. Next, calculate the price for each of these categories (and any other that may arise), then add them all up and add a small amount to cover unforeseen expenses.

You may wish to give an itemized list to your client when you present an estimate. Each vendor or supplier should be shown separately. Give a description of the services you're offering and the price for each. This is a great way to remind clients that you will only receive a fraction of the service fee.

CHAPTER 9

8 Key Elements to Event Planning that Will Make Your Event a Great Success

Every event requires a plan and a process to reach your goals. It is difficult to host an event. It is even more challenging to achieve your goals. These eight essential elements will ensure that your event is a success.

1. Learn the purpose of the Event

Each event should have a primary purpose, goals, and objectives. These are the measures of success. Knowing the purpose of an event will help you plan better and allocate your time and money more effectively. To achieve success, you must set realistic goals and a realistic attendance goal. This leads us to the next point.

2. Know your Audience

You need to determine your target audience and what

their needs are, depending on your organisation's goals. Once you have identified your target audience, you need to determine where they are located and how you will reach them. Are you able to get enough prospects?

There are many options to reach your prospects and to generate more potential clients and audiences. There are many ways to reach your prospects, including email marketing, telemarketing and social media. Depending on the target audience, some methods will be more effective than others.

You can also determine what type of events to host by gathering all the information you can about your audience.

3. It is crucial to choose the right venue

The type of event you are hosting, and the target audience will determine which venue is best for your event. It is essential to establish a link between the organization's expectations, the venue chosen and the audience.

4. The timing of an event is just as important as the right venue. Many factors need to be taken into consideration when determining the timing of an event. These include the days of the week, months of the year, holidays, other events, type of event, and location.

5. Now that you have a clear goal and know your audience, it's time to create a plan for executing the tasks to achieve the goal. You should plan, depending on how complex or large the event is. This will allow you to have enough time to fully understand the details, the requirements and the necessary actions. Before you start planning, it is essential to identify the key milestones and deadlines. Planning an event is only part of the equation. You must also follow the timeline and keep track.

6. Make sure your content is appealing to your target

audience

It is essential to think about the value that attendees will get from attending your event. Make compelling content that appeals to your target audience. Give the information your audience needs or solve their problems. Don't sell your business by merely delivering sales pitches.

Engage your audience by being creative in creating content. Check out some of the best new techniques that event organizers, exhibitors are using to increase attendee engagement and generating better ROI.

7. Create the message that you want to spread through the event

It's a great way to achieve your event objectives. This gives you the chance to communicate your message in a way that the audience can understand and agree with. Events are not just for cheering up participants. They should also achieve their mission to help the audience understand the organization's contribution and impact. This makes it easy for attendees to trust the organization.

8. The main goal of B2B events likely is to capture leads from potential prospects. It will be easier to generate leads if you take care of the above. However, you must plan how you are going to capture your information. You can think of creative ways or mechanisms that will work best for your event. You can even manage your events through our online meeting without any hurdles regardless of these above elements.

CHAPTER 10

Are you planning a corporate event or meeting? These eight tips will make sure it runs smoothly

It can be challenging to plan a corporate event. Here are eight tips from professionals to make sure your event runs smoothly.

Event management and leadership are two of the most demanding and fast-paced challenges any professional could face. These events require creativity, time management and total concentration. You must find ways to simplify your schedule, collaborate effectively and avoid making mistakes. This will ensure your guests have a memorable experience.

1) Reduce the complexity of ticketing

Many event leaders have adopted Eventbrite and Billetto

as their ticketing platforms of choice. These services are easy to use and integrate with email and social media.

Although QR code ticketing is not the future, there are more straightforward ways to register digitally via tablet or device. This will allow you to save time and help people get into the venue quicker.

2) Manage your project digitally

It's a hassle trying to keep track of a constantly growing inbox. To help you keep project-to-project communication separate and precise, it's worth investing in digital project management software such as Basecamp.

This will keep your team informed about the progress of the event and allows for closer collaboration. You can include clients in threads to make it easy for them to get updates and answer questions.

3) Start with "Why."

As set out in Simon Sinek's fantastic book on corporate culture, creating something useful, desirable and popular requires you to 'start with why.'

Your event will be more appealing if you understand the motivations behind your actions and communicate them to your attendees.

4) Choose the right venue

Finding the right venue is key. Finding the right corporate venue in London or elsewhere is a challenge. Before you go on-site, be sure to have a list of your requirements. Ask the venue management series of questions. They may have facilities you didn't know about, or they might be unwilling to discuss areas that are not available.

When looking at venues, it is crucial to consider logistics. Are there enough toilets available for everyone? In some cases, you can use a portable toilet hire company to add a few more facilities. You will need to confirm with the venue management if they have the space and allow you to do this. You don't want your guests to have to find parking problems when they arrive at the event. Make sure you know how many people will be attending the event and ensure enough parking.

Also, make sure to check the entrances of the venue. This will ensure that everything is accessible. You may need to bring stands and stages. Access is essential to ensure that everything can be set up quickly. Explore the options and be curious to find the best venue of your choice.

5) Keep it fresh

It can be challenging to keep things fresh, interesting, and balanced when organising an event like a conference or corporate outing. There are many speakers to hear, workshops to attend, and activities that need to be coordinated.

You can only achieve balance by identifying the learning threads that run through the day and balancing the foster of these takeaways with practical requirements of the venue and your attendees.

6) Remember lights, camera, action!

Lighting can seem like an afterthought to many, but it can make or break your event's perception. Learning the hard way is not the best way to learn. Leaving lighting to last is like curating a gallery without first looking at the art. If the podium is too bright or the audience cannot read their notes, it can compromise the atmosphere, structure, and functionality of your event.

It's essential to allow videographers and photographers to work in the appropriate space. Lighting is a crucial consideration when planning your event venue. This will ensure that everyone has what they need to make it a success.

7) Influence the influencers

Ensure you provide all the necessary items for speakers, panellists, or special guests at your event. It is a good idea to send a thank-you package to the speakers, panellists and special guests after the event. You don't need to send anything extravagant, but it should be a sincere expression of gratitude and appreciation for their contributions.

8) Continue the conversation

The event does not end with the last guest leaving. A 'legacy plan for the next event is an integral part of proving that events are valuable to your company or community. Sharing presentations and giving actionable tips is one thing. But, it is vital to continue the conversation. You can use video resources to keep the momentum going, such as reaction blogs, videos of attendees and even spin-off events.

CHAPTER 11

Creative Ways Event Planners can Find New Clients

Event planning is never complete without finding new clients. Prospects must be reached while you manage the work on your already-booked events. You must be different from your competition. How can you draw potential clients to your business in a creative manner? These are five ideas to help you attract potential clients.

1. Offer experiences

People desire more than just a formal event. People want stories and experiences to share with their family and friends (primarily via social networks). Are you able to offer experiences as part of your events? You might consider combining your events with workshops, classes, demonstrations or exceptional food or drink tastings or other activities. Look at the latest trends like beer yoga, cooking classes and escape rooms to see which would work best for your clients.

2. People hire you to manage their events because you are an expert in what you do. You can show off your knowledge by writing a blog or sharing your thoughts on industry news and trends via email or social media. You don't have to reveal all your secrets. Prospective clients will be impressed and begin to recognize you for being an expert. Search engines will index the information that you share online. Your business will be more likely to show up in searches that seek experts on the topics you write.

3. Get involved with the local blogging community.

You might also consider reaching out to famous bloggers in your area to promote what you do. You can think about it this way; Bloggers who write about weddings and food or local events would be interested in your services, and you could introduce your business directly to their readers. You can search for bloggers in your local area who write on these topics and hold an event to showcase what you have to offer in return for a mention on their blogs and social media.

4. Assist Nonprofits

Volunteering to help nonprofits with events is a win-win. You help people in need and show that you are investing in your community. You'll also meet many people during the planning and the actual event. When they search for event planners, you'll be top on their minds.

5. You may have noticed that social media is becoming more popular for live streaming. It works. Social media users watch live videos three times longer than prerecorded videos. They're also 1.7 times more

likely to buy the product or services mentioned in the video. Use the live streaming tools on Facebook, Instagram, Twitter, LinkedIn and YouTube to promote your business. Showcase what is happening at an event, answer questions or give helpful tips.

The Top 7 Personality Traits that Make a Great Event Manager

Event managers who are successful at their peak have been driven and organized professionals. But did they start that way? These are the traits that you may have if you want to be one. They could also be the innate qualities you possess, making you the ideal person for event management.

1. Amazing communication skills

Communication takes many forms throughout the day. For most of us, it happens in almost all communication channels. Your abilities in speaking, listening, reading, writing, signalling, and presenting can make a big difference in the success of event management.

Martin Turner, Senior Lecturer at Event Academy, comments that "it's vital to be a phenomenal communicator both oral and written" This is good news for people who are natural communicators and can communicate clearly and concisely. But it doesn't stop there. It's more than just communicating information between people. In events, it's about being able to communicate and present ideas.

2. Being a people person is important Team Player

Communication is a natural part of communication. It includes the ability to communicate effectively with others. This includes being approachable and able to work in groups. Justine Kane, Event Academy Course Director, says that such people skills are important at all levels of expertise and in any position within the pack. Event managers must be *leaders and* team members.

It is important to communicate with and be part of larger teams to succeed at events. Respect and patience are key personal characteristics that underpin this umbrella of communication and teamwork. When working with professionals in busy teams, patience is as important as pro-activity. It's part of respecting their professionalism. Respect is shown by being patient and waiting for the agreed deadlines and actions. Also, you show respect by being punctual and prompt with your responses and actions. This is part of being a team player *with all those involved* if you are organizing and the network that supports it. Not just the employer or client who pays for it.

3. Flexibility, Willingness and a Positive Attitude

Your attitude is what can make or break your event manager career. Flexibility and adaptability are essential. There is no place for monomindedness. You need to be flexible and adaptable to all the tasks an event manager may perform.

4. Highly organized and efficient

The events industry is a business that relies on organisational skills. It is a market where success is given. Project management is all about organization and logic.

5. Budgeting Capability

Experts agree that being able to manage budgets is crucial to your success. While a natural ability for numbers is a plus, it's possible to learn skills that will help you manage your budget and negotiate effectively.

6. Pay attention to detail and take pride in your work

It is essential to have the personal qualities of being able to pay attention to details and taking pride in what you do. Your satisfaction is crucial to the success of the event as well as your role.

7. Stamina and determination to succeed, will power to work hard

You can only deliver significant events if you have the determination and drive. These are not externally motivating, but they aren't something you can teach.

Chirag Patel, a graduate of Event Academy, recalls from his event studies how determination helped him to create a career in events. "At the end, it all comes down to each individual to make strides and push themselves forwards to get their foot in front of the door. This is the most difficult thing to do."

However, a determination is more than a characteristic that gets you started. To be a successful event professional, you must also have the ability to work hard and persevere. According to Chirag, this industry is high-pressure and requires something more. It all comes down to the mindset you adopt. It's not about being enthusiastic and driven, but it's also about being calm under pressure. The people who succeed in this field have a strong drive and a strong mentality.

NOTE: Of course, any SWOT analysis will demonstrate that we all have weaknesses, and whilst it's a must-have attribute in many students and teams, it is widely acknowledge that: "There's no chance that you're going to have all of them because there's no such thing as the perfect person - and therefore, no such thing as the perfect event manager." This is why, if you find your personality isn't yet a great match, to make the most of event management training courses, which directly support the development of industry-essential personal skills. Confidence is one example. It's a trait that supports all the others and can be developed through event experience and training.

CHAPTER 12

How to Get Experience in Event Planning With Tips

Even though event planning can seem overwhelming, one-person event managers can still be as valuable as larger companies. Clients require people who can demonstrate their abilities and who can adapt to their events. You don't need event planning experience to get started in your dream job.

How to plan events without any experience

These 12 strategies will help you grow your event management career, find new clients, and improve your experience.

1. Get an education

You might consider pursuing a degree in event planning or another similar field. There are many degrees available to professional event managers that can teach you the skills necessary for your future career in event management. Some relevant college degrees include:

- **Management of a hotel or restaurant:** This degree will allow you to master the essentials of managing large-scale events and best practices in guest management. It also gives you an introduction to the catering business.

- **Marketing:** A strong marketer is required to manage significant events. They must be able to attract guests, coordinate promotional events, and keep the message consistent.

- **Public relations:** Public relations professionals are the link between the public and organizations. They often play a major role in developing and marketing events to increase awareness. This degree will give you practical skills in leadership, people management, and attracting the public. It also helps to build business relationships with subcontractors. An education could improve your marketability and show that you have the necessary skills.

2. Earn professional certifications

You might also find classes or professional certifications at your local university in event planning. You can also pursue professional certifications such as these at your local college or university.

- *Certified Meeting Professional (CMP):* The Convention Industry Council (CIC) developed it.

- *Certified Special Events Professional (CSEP):* The International Live Events Association (ILEA) suggests this.

- *Certified in Exhibition Management (CEM):* The International Association of Exhibitions and

Events manages the event.

3. Find your niche

You need to identify your niche and decide what area of event planning you are interested in. Event planning is a broad field that includes fundraisers and stockholder retreats to children's birthday parties and fundraising. You can choose to specialize in almost any type of event. You should be flexible to work with all clients, especially when you're just starting, but you should also focus on your strengths and interests so that you can build expertise in specific areas. Find your niche by identifying the events that you are most passionate about and then tailor your search to those events.

A niche can help you increase your marketability. Businesses and organizations looking for the best event planners can find you by showing interest in the topic. If you are passionate about corporate retreat planning, your portfolio and experience will show that you are the best choice for retreat management.

4. Social media is a great way to engage online

To meet other event planners and experienced planners, join online groups. Employers looking for digital skills will find you more marketable if you have a strong online presence.

5. Participate in local events

Local events offer a unique opportunity to learn and observe event planning, whether they are corporate fundraisers or corporate events. You can gain a unique insight into the logistics and guest experience by attending an event as a guest. You can observe how events are organized, the use of space, the vendors used, and what resources are used. To ask questions and make connections in the industry, you can also meet the event planners.

6. After your better understanding as regard the event planning industry, it is time to research some of the top industry leaders and learn about their experience and qualifications. Contact people who have connections to larger companies if you meet them at events. You can find the names and businesses of industry leaders and ask them for help.

7. Find a mentor

Mentors are more experienced individuals who can guide you in your career. Look out for people with the same qualifications as you. Ask them to mentor your event planning career.

Respect your mentor's time and listen to what they have to say. You might have unique connections, training or access to resources.

8. Volunteer for local organizations

Volunteering at local events is a great way to gain

valuable experience. There are many ways to volunteer your skills, including through awareness campaigns or fundraisers that local charities and nonprofits run.

Volunteering to plan or assist with the event's setup can give you valuable experience and knowledge. Even simple tasks like checking in people and passing out names tags can provide practical experience that you can use to pitch potential clients.

You can volunteer to help organize the events for your local club or organization. These events allow you to show your leadership skills and logistical management skills, as well as vendor relationships.

9. Craft a stellar portfolio

To impress potential clients, create a portfolio that highlights your skills, experience, and niche expertise. These are some suggestions for creating a portfolio.

- **All types of events are possible:** Consider the neighbourhood block parties, garage sales, and multi-family birthday parties that you might have planned. Please describe the role you played and how it impacted the event. Choose the most relevant events to allow clients to see how your experience matches their requirements.

- **Include hard data:** You can show the impact of your event by sharing numbers such as the number of people who attended, the money raised from tickets, or the money donated. The statistics can show how efficient your event planning skills are.

- **Send us photos and videos:** Visuals show your decor and guest experience. You can show the client pictures or videos to help them imagine how their event could look under your direction.

- **Get feedback:** Ask someone to review your

portfolio and provide feedback about its structure and clarity. Your portfolio should be grammatically correct and well-organized.

Create a website

You can promote your services by creating a website. It will also give a glimpse of your style and skills. To ensure the best possible client experience, consider the following elements:

- **Use the contact form:** You can also include your business contact information, such as your email address and phone number, but you can also create a digital form that potential clients can fill out. The form may ask for their contact information and the type of event they are looking for. It can also provide any additional details that will help you prepare for your meeting.

- **Publish your portfolio:** Your website allows

clients to view past events and learn more about you as a planner. It is easier to connect with clients by having it where they can reach you for a quote and meeting.

- **Create a blog:** A blog allows you to share your views on the industry, discuss your successes and challenges, and interact with other event planning bloggers. SEO techniques can make you more visible in the industry by making your blog well-read and reaching more clients.

- **Connect your website to social networks:** Add your social media handles to your website and link to them. If you have photos, clients can also navigate to your social media accounts to view more evidence of your event planning.

10. Event management companies are available

You can still apply to local event management companies

to get more experience, even if your goal is to own your own event management company in the future. You can search social media and online job boards for opportunities to find planner positions at companies that offer the best growth prospects. To determine if a company's reputation is exemplary for you, research the past events and reviews to find out if they can align with your niche.

You may also be eligible to apply for jobs in marketing, advertising and public relations. These roles often involve organizing employee or public events. These and other event management roles can help you learn new skills, keep updated with the latest event trends, and make new connections.

11. Start your own business

These are just a few of the many ways to start your business and get your first client.

- **Use your local network:** Tell your friends, family, and coworkers about your new business. Ask them if they know of anyone who may need an event planner.

- **To find clients, search social media and on job boards:** Search online for clients looking for private event planners. Follow up with them by sending polite emails or call, if you are able.

- **Advertise your website:** Consider marketing to increase your website's visibility and promote it.

- **Create a solid business plan:** Your business plan should include information about your niche, target clients, and your company's mission. Write a description of your employees and the organizational structure if you have them. To show clients your payment expectations, be sure to include a pricing plan that provides for subcontractors, servers, and movers. A professional plan will help you streamline the contract negotiation process and present a complete pitch to clients.

12. Pitch Your Client.

These are some things you should consider when pitching your client.

Do your research: Research the needs of your client based on the job description or information you have about them. You can start planning for your client by researching ahead of time. This will show that you are proactive and collaborative in meeting their needs.

Personalize your meeting: Do some research on social media to find common interests if you are familiar with the client or interviewer before the meeting. You can build a more friendly relationship by sharing common interests, which can help make meetings more enjoyable for both of you. To show your commitment to meeting client expectations, you can ask questions about the company and their needs.

Emphasize your uniqueness: Interviews should highlight the skills that make you stand out as an event planner. Make it clear that you are a great fundraiser. If you are passionate about welcoming environments and social mixing, then identify how you can do this and how it will benefit the client's event. Showing the client/interviewer how your skills and experience match their needs will convince them that you are the right person to fill the position.

CHAPTER 13

The 5 C's Of Event Management
Everybody Should Know

One of the most exciting careers in event management. The average event planner is a busybody in charge of creating an excellent experience for attendees.

Event management is a great career option, but it can be challenging. If you want to be successful in event management, you need to know what you are doing. This is why you need to be familiar with the five C's of Event Management. You can do a lot if you are creative and willing to take on event management. However, there are still many things you can do to make your event a success. These tips are also known as the Five C's and are:

1. Planning a successful event starts with the

concept. The event's purpose should be the first thing you think about. One of the best ways is to think about the most outstanding concerts ever held. Even if you are not hosting a show, this will give you an idea of what you want attendees to feel. You will always have fond memories of an event you attended. This is what you want for your event.

Consider *why* you are organizing this event. What's the purpose of the event. It is possible to host an event for others. Perhaps the event will raise money for a charity. Maybe this is a seminar on a specific subject. Once you know the "why", you can then determine who the event is intended to reach, your target audience should be able to enjoy and benefit from your event. This will allow you to decide what the event should include - speakers, entertainment, activities, catering, and so forth. You must also decide when and where to hold it.

2. Coordinating

We hope you know how to properly plan a schedule. Once you have created your event, the next step is to coordinate it. This includes deciding on a theme for the event. Once you have chosen a theme, you can plan the venue and decorations, as well as any other needs such as hiring speakers or using audio/visual equipment.

It is essential to reserve the venue and date well in advance. If you don't find the right time or location, be flexible with the date and venue. Once you have confirmed the details, you can start advertising the event to potential attendees. This is the stage where you assign tasks to your team members. Reaching out to performers and speakers is one example of these tasks. You may also need to rent or purchase the equipment and technology you require. It is possible to ask your team to coordinate transportation, catering and marketing.

You also need to sit down with an accountant/bookkeeper

to decide the event budget. Make sure to check with the accountant/bookkeeper that no one is exceeding their budget.

3. This stage is often overlooked and neglected in event management. It is easier to manage this stage if you run through the entire event.

You want everything to be on schedule. You should check that there is enough space to accommodate all confirmed guests. Also, check if the venue has enough space for catering companies to set up their food.

It is important to stay on top of all details and be prepared for any changes. Do you have a backup speaker in case a speaker is faulty? Have you created a list of alternate options in case the caterers encounter problems? What can you do if your budget is tight? To ensure that your event is successful, you must consider the worst-case scenario.

4. Culmination

This is the "D-Day". This is the day that the event takes place. This is the day you and your team must be at the top of things.

It is important to create an event itinerary that will be accessible to all participants. Everyone must have access to the venue before the event starts. This will allow you to set up the event and practice the drills before it begins.

You must ensure that the event's progress is monitored and that the schedule is being followed. You must ensure that the other speaker is available for their speech if they are speaking. You must to ensure that caterers are properly preparing food so that guests can check-in. You must be alert throughout the event.

5. Closeout

There is still much to do after the event has ended. It is important to ensure that all payments and terminations of contracts with vendors, caterers, speakers, and others are completed. All payments and terminations of contracts with vendors, caterers, speakers, etc., are complete.

Your team should also be given feedback. Let them know if they did a good job and be given an appraiser. Make sure you let them know if there were any problems so they can improve your next event. Make sure to reach out and thank the performers, vendors, as well as caterers. Ask them what they thought of the event and what they would change. Reach out to your attendees as well and get their feedback.

Acknowledgments

The Glory of this book success goes to God Almighty and my beautiful Family, Fans, Readers & well-wishers, Customers and Friends for their endless support and encouragements.